THIS IS
WHAT I SEE

by stepro books

This is
what I see

"I never have taken a picture I've intended. They're always better or worse."
— Diane Arbus

I ASK NOT ONLY THAT MY CITY,
BUT ALL, GIVE THEMSELVES
TO THE ESSENCE OF OUR CULT –
THE RITUAL ASSEMBLY OF AN
INTERESTED COTERIE IN A SPACE
WHERE MAGIC CAN BE MADE
AND MIRACLES OCCUR.

...from the housing crash in the US, the business hangover from the collapse of Yugoslavia, it's so much undeveloped as it is stuck in a time that was said to have stopped existing. Only, it didn't. People live here. Time moves on and the grass grows and dries in the cracks of the craggy parking lot.

There is a very odd air about the place. In a city known for cafes there isn't a single one in sight. There is no kiosk, grocery store, nor a hair salon. All of which I've come to know as the ubiquitous pieces of Zagreb's geography. Cafes, kiosks, hair salons, and bakeries are to Zagreb what the sand